The Law and Other Essays on Manifestation

©2011 Wilder Publications

Wilder Publications, Inc.
PO Box 10641
Blacksburg, VA 24063

ISBN 10: 1-61720-278-9
ISBN 13: 978-1-61720-278-0

First Edition

10 9 8 7 6 5 4 3 2 1

The Law: and Other Essays on Manifestation

Neville Goddard

Contents

The Law. 5

Be What You Wish; Be What You Believe. 11

By Imagination We Become. 15

The Law of Assumption. 19

Truth. 23

At Your Command. 26

The Law

The whole vast world is no more than man's imagining pushed out. I must qualify that by saying that the world outside of man is dead, but Man is a living soul, and it responds to man, yet man is sound asleep and does not know it. The Lord God placed man in a profound sleep, and as he sleeps the world responds as in a dream, for Man does not know he is asleep, and then he moves from a state of sleep where he is only a living soul to an awakened state where he is a life-giving Spirit. And now he can himself create, for everything is responding to an activity in man which is Imagination. "The eternal body of man is all imagination; that is God himself." (Blake)

Three wonderful case histories were given to me last Tuesday and I can best describe what I mean by telling you of one of them. Here is this lady driving east on Sunset and she comes to a stop at Laurel Canyon. A bus is to her right, and then she sees this little elderly lady in grey who is running diagonally across the street through traffic, trying to catch that bus. The bus driver sees her but he pulls out leaving her on the street. The lady, who gave me this story, told me that she felt compassion for this elderly lady, but she was not in a lane where she could give her a lift; she had to pull out with her line when the light changed. She said to herself, 'I will give that lady a lift just the same.' So in Imagination, she opens her car door and lets her in.

Then still in her Imagination, she hears the lady tell her that she is meeting some friends a few blocks away and if she had to wait for another bus she is afraid they would not wait for her. The lady in the car carried on this imaginary conversation and it took maybe a half a minute until she felt satisfied about it. Four blocks ahead, as she again stopped for a light, someone tapped on the car window, and here stands a breathless little elderly with gray hair dressed in gray. My friend lowered the window and the little lady said 'I have missed my bus. Can you give me a lift? Friends are waiting for me and when they see I do not get off the bus they may go on and leave me.' My friend let her get into the car and then six blocks further the little lady said. 'There are my friends!' and thanks the driver and gets out.

Now here is a lady whom I say is awake. And may I tell you that in Heaven there was joy because one called a sinner (we are all sinners, for we are all missing the mark, and the mark is to awaken) has discovered that the whole world is responsive to what we are thinking. She could not actually give the first little lady a lift so she did it in Imagination, and then she sees this other elderly lady and gives her a lift. Here she is enacting her imaginary drama, and four blocks later when the dream is completed this little ole lady taps at her car window. In her imagination she gave a lift to a little grey haired lady dressed in gray. Does it matter if it was the lady behind at the last bus stop or this lady dressed in gray? Everyone is responding to what we are doing in our Imagination. There is no outside world that is really alive. It depends, for its aliveness, on the activity of man who is a living soul. Man named the animals, the birds, the trees, everything. God became man as a living soul, but He had to forget He was God to become man, and now man has to become a life-giving spirit, where he knows that everything is an imaginal activity.

Here, at that corner where the first part of this little drama took place, half of those who witnessed it would bawl out the bus driver for not waiting for the old lady, and the other half would say she was a fool for running into the street. This lady in the car could have reacted like that, for the dreamer does not know that he is dreaming. It is only when we awake they know they are causing the dream, or even had a dream. The lady in the car saw only someone who had failed to realize an objective, so she enacted a scene for her, implying she had realized it. And four blocks later she meets a little old lady who says to her the exact words she had heard in her Imagination. Her Imaginary dream unfolds in detail. An awakened dream is crystallized in the world. 'Real are the dreams of gods, as they slowly pass their pleasure in a long immortal dream.' When man completely awakens he dreams his pleasure and everything responds while he dreams it.

We think everything in the world is completely independent from our perception of it, but the whole thing is dead. I see it, and come upon it, but the whole thing is dead.' frozen. Then I start an activity within me and then the world that was dead becomes alive, but not knowing I am doing it, I am sound asleep and then the whole thing takes over and it becomes a nightmare. But I must keep control and know it is dependant on me. The world is infinite response and the thing that makes it alive is the living soul called generic man (male-female). And then God wove Himself into the brain of this generic man, and then He sleeps. As man begins to awaken he controls and takes over, and is no longer a victim of his vision, so he has control of his attention. Everyone is free to create his world as he wants it if he knows that the whole thing is responding to him.

In Luke 13 we are told the story of five Galileans who have been murdered by Pilate. 'And he mixed their blood with their offering, etc.' And the central figure of the gospels which is your awakened Imagination says to his followers; 'Do you think these five were worse sinners than the others? I tell you 'No.' But unless you repent you will all likewise perish in the same manner.'Here on one level we think it served them right, just as those who saw the scene on the Sunset Blvd. would say 'It served her right cutting across the street like that!' In this story in Luke we are told that a man sinned in the past and was murdered by Pilate. It has nothing to do with it. Then Jesus asked them, 'Do you think that the eighteen upon whom the tower in Siloam fell and killed them were worse offenders than the others who dwell in Jerusalem? I tell you, No; but unless you repent you will all likewise perish.

On this level of the dream people think of getting even. It is a dream of confusion and people are reactivating, but man has to awaken and become an actor. On this present level man is always reflecting life, not knowing he is the cause of all he observes. But when he awakens from the dream and then becomes an actor. What percentage would have done what this lady in the car did? They would have reacted, or feasted on the fruit of the tree of good and evil. They would have had a violent reaction, and then they would have had a violent resistance from this dead universe. But this lady makes her dream and the whole thing comes to pass exactly as she pictured it, even to the number of blocks. You might almost think she had manufactured that little old lady in gray, but I tell you everything comes in response to our own wonderful imaginal activity.

You can be anything in this world but you cannot know it or expect it to come unless you Act. If you react based on the past, you continue in the same pattern. To be the man you desire to be you must create the scene, as this lady did, and the whole world will be convulsed if that is necessary to bring it to pass. There is no other power but God, but God had to 'forget' he was God in this state of sleep, and then He awakens and consciously determines the conditions he wants in the world.

So again I say to this lady, the angels rejoiced over your awakening, and 'I say this without pride' they also rejoiced because I kept my promise that I would come and awaken this sleeper in the world of men. For I, also, had to forget everything to become man. For when one goes and then returns he has to forget everything to become man. For when one goes, and then returns he has to forget everything, but he promises he will carry out his pledge and help man awaken. Then the living soul becomes a life-giving spirit, and then creates.

Take it seriously. Do not go through this with your dream un-acted. It took this lady 30 seconds to enact her drama and another 60 seconds to realize it. You tell yourselves -it must take time- What time? Read Corinthians 1:18, I could go before men with all the words of wisdom, but know only one thing, the cross. To the wise it is foolishness, etc. What is the cross? Think of it in this light. You began, seemingly in your mother's womb and end in the grave. You do not, but you have that picture. Look on the horizontal line of the cross as time. Intersecting this vertical line and call that infinite states, like Jacobs ladder. At any section of time I can move up or down. Time is flowing and the state with which I am identified still unfolds.

So, while seated in my car I can move up and enact a drama. I acted and remained within that state. It unfolded. It took 60 seconds. There are infinite states intersecting the line of time. We become one with a certain state and it demonstrates itself in actual phenomena. Everyone here, it need not take you more than 30 seconds to bring about a change of state. What would it be like? And you name your desire. Remain in that state, and that state, by the passage of time, will unfold in your world. You do nothing about it once you have entered the state'for the outer must move by compulsion of the inner power.

This little lady in gray had to come to my friend's car. Every detail of that imaginary act took place.

Why not? The universe is infinite response. When you know that there is no one in the whole world could ever faze you, because he is a shadow. I have seen the whole world dead, completely frozen, and then I allowed something within me to start and everything became animated. Then you ask yourself a million questions. Who am I? What is it all about? Why? Everything here is responding to the imaginal activity within man.

When someone who is sick becomes well: when someone who is blind then sees, is that more of a miracle than what this lady told? She is awake. If you make a fortune it means nothing. All the honors of men in a state of sleep are as nothing. You must 'repent.' It has nothing to do with the so-called judgment of God. It is only a dream and man is reacting to the dream and he does not know that he is the dreamer and causing all the dream.

The literal meaning of the Greek word translated as repent means 'a change of mind.' It has nothing to do with the moral picture. The churches introduced that, but it has nothing to do with it. I don't care what a man has done, if he changes his mind in this meaning of the word 'repent' things will change, for he is then on the line of vertical line of states. He stands at a point on the states. There are infinite states and we must learn to distinguish between the state and the individual occupying the state. But I can now change and move into another state. I can in Time, do it in a split second and rise on the vertical line of the states.

So, 'I come, only to teach the cross," said Paul. I will rise within myself and ignore the former state, and within myself I will assume that things are as I want them to be. If I remain faithful, the passage of Time will unfold it. So, Blake said, 'Eternity is in love with the productions of Time.' I tell you, do not let anyone ever convince you that because of your past accomplishments or your present state in the world that you cannot change your position by rising within yourself, and then see the whole world respond. And I mean NOW!

So, I tell you this lady is awake; the Child is awake in her, the purpose of life is to awake. If the whole vast world or sleeping humanity thought her important, would she feel flattered? If in a dream everyone praised you and then you awoke and found it was all a dream, would you be flattered? One dreamer puts a medal on another dreamer, and they do not know it. It is only the awakening that is important. Awakening and doing the will of God. God's will is in you active as your own Imagination, and His will is to realize the imaginal state. To realize something novel as this lady did or to maintain something to maintain in being, or to let things go that you feel are unlovely. I will do it all and only act, and stop re-acting. Then the whole book, The Bible, becomes alive. Leave all the 'wise men to mock it or tolerate.' Let them reach the moon or the stars, they are all dead. Nothing lives outside of man. Man is the living soul, turning slowly into a life-giving Spirit. But you cannot tell it except in a parable or metaphor to excite the mind of man to get him to go out and prove it.

Leave the good and evil and eat of the Tree of Life. Nothing in the world is untrue if you want it to be true. You are the truth of everything that you perceive. 'I am the truth, and the way, the life revealed.' If I have physically nothing in my pocket, then in Imagination I have MUCH. But that is a lie based on fact, but truth is based on the intensity of my imagination and then I will create it in my world. Should I accept facts and use them as to what I should imagine? No.

It is told us in the story of the fig tree. It did not bear for three years. One said, 'Cut it down, and throw it away.' But the keeper of the vineyard pleaded NO'! Who is the tree? I am the tree; you are the tree. We bear or we do not. But the Keeper said he would dig around the tree and feed it 'or manure it, as we would say today' and see if it will not bear. Well I do that here every week and try to get the tree 'you' me to bear. You should bear whatever you desire. If you want to be happily married, you should be. The world is only response. If you want money, get it. Everything is a dream anyway. When you awake and know what you are creating and that you are creating it that is a different thing.

The greatest book is the Bible, but it has been taken from a moral basis and it is all weeping and tears. It seems almost ruthless as given to us in the Gospel, if taken literally. The New Testament interprets the Old Testament, and it has nothing to do with morals. You change your mind and stay in that changed state until it unfolds. Man thinks he has to work himself out of something, but it is God asleep in you as a living soul, and then we are reborn as a life-giving spirit. We do it here in this little classroom called Earth or beyond the grave, for you cannot die. You can be just as asleep beyond the grave. I meet them constantly, and they are just like this. Same loves and same hates. No change. They will go through it until they finally awake, until they cease to re-act and begin to act.

Do not take this story lightly which I have told you tonight. Take it to heart. Tonight when you are driving home enact a scene. No matter what it is. Forget good and evil. Enact a scene that implies you have what you desire, and to the degree that you are faithful to that state, it will unfold in your world and no power can stop it, for there is no other power.

Nothing is independent of your perception of it, and this goes for that great philosopher among us who is still claiming that everything is independent of the perceiver, but that the perceiver has certain powers. It is not so. Nothing is independent of the perceiver. Everything is 'burned up' when I cease to behold it. It may exist for another, but not for me.

Let us make our dream a noble one, for the world is infinite response to you, the being you want to be.

Now let us go into the silence.

Be What You Wish; Be What You Believe

A newspaperman related to me that our great scientist, Robert Millikan, once told him that he had set a goal for himself at an early age when he was still very poor and unproven in the great work he was to do in the future. He condensed his dream of greatness and security into a simple statement, which statement, implied that his dream of greatness and security was already realized. Then he repeated the statement over and over again to himself until the idea of greatness and security filled his mind and crowded all other ideas out of his consciousness. These may not have been the words of Dr. Millikan but they are those given to me and I quote, "I have a lavish, steady, dependable income, consistent with integrity and mutual benefit." As I have said repeatedly, everything depends upon our attitude towards ourselves. That which we will not affirm as true of ourselves cannot develop in our life. Dr. Millikan wrote his dream of greatness and security in the first person, present tense. He did not say, "I will be great; I will be secure," for that would have implied that he was not great and secure. Instead, he made his future dream a present fact. "I have," said he, "a lavish, steady, dependable income, consistent with integrity and mutual benefit."

The future dream must become a present fact in the mind of him who seeks to realize it. We must experience in imagination what we would experience in reality in the event we achieved our goal, for the soul imagining itself into a situation takes on the results of that imaginary act. If it does not imagine itself into a situation, it is ever free of the result.

It is the purpose of this teaching to lift us to a higher state of consciousness, to stir the highest in us to confidence and self-assertion, for that which stirs the highest in us is our teacher and healer. The very first word of correction or cure is always, "Arise." If we are to understand the reason for this constant command of the Bible to "arise," we must recognize that the universe understood internally is an infinite series of levels and man is what he is according to where he is in that series. As we are lifted up in consciousness, our world reshapes itself in harmony with the level to which we are lifted. He who rises from his prayer a better man, his prayer has been granted.

To change the present state we, like Dr. Millikan, must rise to a higher level of consciousness. This rise is accomplished by affirming that we are already that which we want to be; by assuming the feeling of the wish fulfilled. The drama of life is a psychological one which we bring to pass by our attitudes rather than by our acts. There is no escape from our present predicament except by a radical psychological transformation. Everything depends upon our attitude towards ourselves. That which we will not affirm as true of ourselves will not develop in our lives.

We hear much of the humble man, the meek man – but what is meant by a meek man? He is not poor and groveling, the proverbial doormat, as he is generally conceived to be. Men who make themselves as worms in their own sight have lost the vision of that life – into the likeness of which it is the true purpose of the spirit to transform this life. Men should take their measurements not from life as they see it but from men like Dr. Millkan, who, while poor and unproven, dared to assume, "I have a lavish, steady, dependable income, consistent with integrity and mutual benefit." Such men are the meek of the Gospels, the men who inherit the earth. Any concept of self less than the best robs us of the earth. The promise is, "Blessed are the meek, for they shall inherit the earth." In the original text, the word translated as meek is the opposite of the words – resentful – angry. It has the meaning of becoming "tamed" as a wild animal is tamed. After the mind is tamed, it may be likened to a vine, of which it may be said, "Behold this vine. I found it a wild tree whose wanton strength had swollen into irregular twigs. But I pruned the plant, and it grew temperate in its vain expense of useless leaves, and knotted as you see into these clean, full clusters to repay the hand that wisely wounded it."

A meek man is a self-disciplined man. He is so disciplined he sees only the finest, he thinks only the best. He is the one who fulfills the suggestion, "Brethren, whatsoever things are true, whatsoever things are honest, whatsoever things are just, whatsoever things are pure, whatsoever things are lovely, whatsoever things are of good report; if there be any virtue and if there be any praise, think on these things."

We rise to a higher level of consciousness, not because we have curbed our passions, but because we have cultivated our virtues. In truth, a meek man is a man in complete control of his moods, and his moods are the highest, for he knows he must keep a high mood if he would walk with the highest.

It is my belief that all men can, like Dr. Millikan, change the course of their lives. I believe that Dr. Millikan's technique of making his desire a present fact to himself is of great importance to any seeker after the "truth." It is also his high purpose to be of "mutual benefit" that is inevitably the goal of us all. It is much easier to imagine the good of all than to be purely selfish in our imagining. By our imagination, by our affirmations, we can change our world, we can change our future. To the man of high purpose, to the disciplined man, this is a natural measure, so let us all become disciplined men. Next Sunday morning, July 15th, I am speaking as the guest of Dr. Bailes at 10:30 at the Fox-Wilshire Theater on Wilshire Boulevard, near La Cienega. My subject for next Sunday is "Changing Your Future." It is a subject near to the hearts of us all. I hope you will all come on Sunday to learn how to be the disciplined man, the meek man, who "changes his future" to the benefit of his fellow man. If you are observant, you will notice the swift echo or response to your every mood in this message and you will be able to key it to the circumstances of your daily life. When we are certain of the relationship of mood to circumstance in our lives, we welcome what befalls us. We know that all we meet is part of ourselves. In the creation of a new life we must begin at the beginning, with a change of mood. Every high mood of man is the opening of the door to a higher level for him. Let us mould our lives about a high mood or a community of high moods. Individuals, as well as communities, grow spiritually in proportion as they rise to a higher ideal. If their ideal is lowered, they sink to its depths; if their ideal is exalted, they are elevated to heights unimagined. We must keep the high mood if we would walk with the highest; the heights, also, were meant for habitation. All forms of the creative imagination imply elements of feeling. Feeling is the ferment without which no creation is possible. There is nothing wrong with our desire to transcend our present state. There would be no progress in this world were it not for man's dissatisfaction with himself. It is natural for us to seek a more beautiful personal life; it is right that we wish for greater understanding, greater health, greater security. It is stated in the sixteenth chapter of the Gospel of St. John, "Heretofore have ye asked for nothing in my name; ask and ye shall receive, that your joy may be full."

A spiritual revival is needed for mankind, but by spiritual revival I mean a true religious attitude, one in which each individual, himself, accepts the challenge of embodying a new and higher value of himself as Dr. Millikan did. A nation can exhibit no greater wisdom in the mass than it generates in its units. For this reason, I have always preached self-help, knowing that if we strive passionately after this kind of self-help, that is, to embody a new and higher concept of ourselves, then all other kinds of help will be at our service.

The ideal we serve and hope to achieve is ready for a new incarnation; but unless we offer it human parentage it is incapable of birth. We must affirm that we are already that which we hope to be and live as though we were, knowing like Dr. Millikan, that our assumption, though false to the outer world, if persisted in, will harden into fact.

The perfect man judges not after appearances; he judges righteously. He sees himself and others as he desires himself and them to be. He hears what he wants to hear. He sees and hears only the good. He knows the truth, and the truth sets him free and leads him to good. The truth shall set all mankind free. This is our spiritual revival. Character is largely the result of the direction and persistence of voluntary attention.

"Think truly, and thy thoughts shall the world's famine feed;

Speak truly, and each word of thine shall be a fruitful seed;

Live truly, and thy life shall be a great and noble creed."

By Imagination We Become

How many times have we heard someone say, "Oh, it's only his imagination?" Only his imagination - man's imagination is the man himself. No man has too little imagination, but few men have disciplined their imagination. Imagination is itself indestructible. Therein lies the horror of its misuse. Daily, we pass some stranger on the street and observe him muttering to himself, carrying on an imaginary argument with one not present. He is arguing with vehemence, with fear or with hatred, not realizing that he is setting in motion, by his imagination, an unpleasant event which he will presently encounter.

The world, as imagination sees it, is the real world. Not facts, but figments of the imagination, shape our daily lives. It is the exact and literal minded who live in a fictitious world. Only imagination can restore the Eden from which experience has driven us out. Imagination is the sense by which we perceived the above, the power by which we resolve vision into being. Every stage of man's progress is made by the exercise of the imagination. It is only because men do not perfectly imagine and believe that their results are sometimes uncertain when they might always be perfectly certain. Determined imagination is the beginning of all successful operation. The imagination, alone, is the means of fulfilling the intention. The man who, at will, can call up whatever image he pleases is, by virtue of the power of his imagination, least of all subject to caprice. The solitary or captive can, by intensity of imagination and feeling, affect myriads so that he can act through many men and speak through many voices. "We should never be certain," wrote William Butler Yeats in his IDEAS OF GOOD AND EVIL, "that it was not some woman treading in the wine-press who began that subtle change in men's minds, or that the passion did not begin in the mind of some shepherd boy, lighting up his eyes for a moment before it ran upon its way."

Let me tell you the story of a very dear friend of mine, at the time the costume designer of the Music Hall in New York. She told me, one day, of her difficulty in working with one of the producers who invariably criticized and rejected her best work unjustly; that he was often rude and seemed deliberately unfair to her. Upon hearing her story, I reminded her, as I am reminding you, that men can only echo to us that which we whisper to them in secret. I had no doubt but that she silently argued with the producer, not in the flesh, but in quiet moments to herself. She confessed that she did just that each morning as she walked to work. I asked her to change her attitude toward him, to assume that he was congratulating her on her fine designs and she, in turn, was thanking him for his praise and kindness. This young designer took my advice and as she walked to the theater, she imagined a perfect relationship of the producer praising her work and she, in turn, responding with gratitude for his appreciation. This she did morning after morning and in a very short while, she discovered for herself that her own attitude determined the scenery of her existence. The behavior of the producer completely reversed itself. He became the most pleasant professional employer she had encountered. His behavior merely echoed the changes that she had whispered within herself. What she did was by the power of imagination. Her fantasy led his; and she, herself, dictated to him the discourse they eventually had together at the time she was seemingly walking alone.

Let us set ourselves, here and now, a daily exercise of controlling and disciplining our imagination. What finer beginning than to imagine better than the best we know for a friend. There is no coal of character so dead that it will not glow and flame if but slightly turned. Don't blame; only resolve. Life, like music, can by a new setting turn all its discords into harmonies. Represent your friend to yourself as already expressing that which he desires to be. Let us know that with whatever attitude we approach another, a similar attitude approaches us.

How can we do this? Do what my friend did. To establish rapport, call your friend mentally. Focus your attention on him and mentally call his name just as you would to attract his attention were you to see him on the street. Imagine that he has answered, mentally hear his voice – imagine that he is telling you of the great good you have desired for him. You, in turn, tell him of your joy in witnessing his good fortune. Having mentally heard that which you wanted to hear, having thrilled to the news heard, go about your daily task. Your imagined conversation must awaken what it affirmed; the acceptance of the end wills the means. And the wisest reflection could not devise more effective means than those which are willed by the acceptance of the end.

However, your conversation with your friend must be in a manner which does not express the slightest doubt as to the truth of what you imagine that you hear and say. If you do not control your imagination, you will find that you are hearing and saying all that you formerly heard and said. We are creatures of habit; and habit, though not law, acts like the most compelling law in the world. With this knowledge of the power of imagination, be as the disciplined man and transform your world by imagining and feeling only what is lovely and of good report. The beautiful idea you awaken in yourself shall not fail to arouse its affinity in others. Do not wait four months for the harvest. Today is the day to practice the control and discipline of your imagination. Man is only limited by weakness of attention and poverty of imagination. The great secret is a controlled imagination and a well sustained attention, firmly and repeatedly focused on the object to be accomplished.

"Now is the acceptable time to give beauty for ashes, joy for mourning, praise for the spirit of heaviness; that they might be called trees of righteousness, the planting of the Lord that He might be glorified."

Now is the time to control our imagination and attention. By control, I do not mean restraint by will power but rather cultivation through love and compassion. With so much of the world in discord we cannot possibly emphasize too strongly the power of imaginative love. Imaginative Love, that is my subject next Sunday morning when I shall speak for Dr. Bailes while he is on his holiday. The services will be held as always at the Fox Wilshire Theater on Wilshire Boulevard, near La Cienega at 10:30. "As the world is, so is the individual," should be changed to, "As the individual is so is the world." And I hope to be able to bring to each of you present the true meaning of the words of Zechariah, "Speak ye every man the truth to his neighbor and let none of you imagine evil in your hearts against his neighbor." What a wonderful challenge to you and to me. "As a man thinketh in his heart so is he." As a man imagines so is he. Hold fast to love in your imagination. By creating an ideal within your mental sphere you can approximate yourself to this "ideal image" till you become one and the same with it, thereby transforming yourself into it, or rather, absorbing its qualities into the very core of your being. Never, never, lose sight of the power that is within you. Imaginative love lifts the invisible into sight and gives us water in the desert. It builds for the soul its only fit abiding place. Beauty, love and all of good report are the garden, but imaginative love is the way into the garden.

Sow an imaginary conversation, you reap an act;

Sow an act, you reap a habit;

Sow a habit, you reap a character;

Sow a character, you reap your destiny.

By imagination, we are all reaping our destinies, whether they be good, bad, or indifferent. Imagination has full power of objective realization and every stage of man's progress or regression is made by the exercise of imagination. I believe with William Blake, "What seems to be, is, to those to whom it seems to be, and is productive of the most dreadful consequences to those to whom it seems to be, even of torments, despair, and eternal death. By imagination and desire we become what we desire to be. Let us affirm to ourselves that we are what we imagine. If we persist in the assumption that we are what we wish to be, we will become transformed into that which we have imagined ourselves to be. We were born by a natural miracle of love and for a brief space of time our needs were all another's care. In that simple truth lies the secret of life. Except by love, we cannot truly live at all. Our parents in their separate individualities have no power to transmit life. So, back we come to the basic truth that life is the offspring of love. Therefore, no love, no life. Thus, it is rational to say that, "God is Love."

Love is our birthright. Love is the fundamental necessity of our life. "Do not go seeking for that which you are. Those who go seeking for love only make manifest their own lovelessness and the loveless never find love. Only the loving find love and they never have to seek for it."

The Law of Assumption

The great mystic, William Blake, wrote almost two hundred years ago, "What seems to be, is, to those to whom it seems to be and is productive of the most dreadful consequences to those to whom it seems to be." Now, at first, this mystical gem seems a bit involved, or at best to be a play on words; but it is nothing of the kind. Listen to it carefully. "What seems to be, is, to those to whom it seems to be." That is certainly clear enough. It is a simple truth about the law of assumption, and a warning of the consequences of its misuse. The author of the Epistle to the Romans declared in the fourteenth chapter, "I know, and am persuaded by the Lord Jesus, that there is nothing unclean of itself; but to him that esteemeth anything to be unclean, to him it is unclearn."

We see by this that it is not superior insight but purblindness that reads into the greatness of men some littleness with which it chances to be familiar, for what seems to be, is, to those to whom it seems to be.

Experiments recently conducted at two of our leading universities revealed this great truth about the law of assumption. They stated in their releases to the newspapers, that after two thousand experiments they came to the conclusion that, 'What you see when you look at something depends not so much on what is there as on the assumption you make when you look. What you believe to be the real physical world is actually only an assumptive world." In other words, you would not define your husband in the same way that you mother would. Yet, you are both defining the same person. Your particular relationship to a thing influences your feelings with respect to that thing and makes you see in it an element which is not there. If your feeling in the matter is a self-element; it can be cast out. If it is a permanent distinction in the state considered, it cannot be cast out. The thing to do is to try. If you can change your opinion of another, then what you now believe of him cannot be absolutely true, but relatively true.

Men believe in the reality of the external world because they do not know how to focus and condense their powers to penetrate its thin crust. Strangely enough, it is not difficult to penetrate this view of the senses. To remove the veil of the senses, we do not employ great effort; the objective world vanishes as we turn our attention from it. We have only to concentrate on the state desired to mentally see it; but to give reality to it so that it will become an objective fact, we must focus our attention upon the desired state until it has all the sensory vividness and feeling of reality. When, through concentrated attention, our desire appears to possess the distinctness and feeling of reality; when the form of thought is as vivid as the form of nature, we have given it the right to become a visible fact in our lives. Each man must find the means best suited to his nature to control his attention and concentrate it on the desired state. I find for myself the best state to be one of meditation, a relaxed state akin to sleep, but a state in which I am still consciously in control of my imagination and capable of fixing my attention on a mental object.

If it is difficult to control the direction of your attention while in this state akin to sleep, you may find gazing fixedly into an object very helpful. Do not look at its surface, but rather into and beyond any plain object such as a wall, a carpet or any object which possesses depth. Arrange it to return as little reflection as possible. Imagine, then, that in this depth you are seeing and hearing what you want to see and hear until your attention is exclusively occupied by the imagined state.

At the end of your meditation, when you awake from your controlled waking dream you feel as though you had returned from a great distance. The visible world which you had shut out returns to consciousness and, by its very presence, informs you that you have been self-deceived into believing that the object of your contemplation was real; but if you remain faithful to your vision this sustained mental attitude will give reality to your visions and they will become visible concrete facts in your world.

Define your highest ideal and concentrate your attention upon this ideal until you identify yourself with it. Assume the feeling of being it – the feeling that would be yours were you now embodying it in your world. This assumption, though now denied by your senses, "if persisted in" – will become a fact in your world. You will know when you have succeeded in fixing the desired state in consciousness simply by looking mentally at the people you know. This is a wonderful check on yourself as your mental conversations are more revealing than your physical conversations are. If, in your mental conversations with others, you talk with them as you formerly did, then you have not changed your concept of self, for all changes of concepts of self result in a changed relationship to the world. Remember what was said earlier, "What you see when you look at something depends not so much on what is there as on the assumption you make when you look." Therefore, the assumption of the wish fulfilled should make you see the world mentally as you would physically were your assumption a physical fact. The spiritual man speaks to the natural man through the language of desire. The key to progress in life and to the fulfillment of dreams lies in the ready obedience to the voice. Unhesitating obedience to its voice is an immediate assumption of the wish fulfilled. To desire a state is to have it. As Pascal said, "You would not have sought me had you not already found me." Man, by assuming the feeling of the wish fulfilled and then living and acting on this conviction changes his future in harmony with his assumption. To "change his future" is the inalienable right of freedom loving individuals. There would be no progress in the world were it not for the divine discontent in man which urges him on to higher and higher levels of consciousness. I have chosen this subject so close to the hearts of us all - "Changing Your Future" - for my message next Sunday morning. I am to have the great joy of speaking for Dr. Bailes while he is vacationing. The service will be held at 10:30 at the Fox Wilshire Theater on Wilshire Boulevard near La Cienega Boulevard.

Since the right to change our future is our birthright as sons of God, let us accept its challenge and learn just how to do it. Again today, speaking of changing your future, I wish to stress the importance of a real transformation of self - not merely a slight alteration of circumstances which, in a matter of moments, will permit us to slip back into the old dissatisfied man. In your meditation, allow others to see you as they would see you were this new concept of self a concrete fact. You always seem to others the embodiment of the ideal you inspire. Therefore, in meditation, when you contemplate others, you must be seen by them mentally as you would be seen by them physically were your conception of yourself an objective fact. That is, in meditation, you imagine that they see you expressing this nobler man you desire to be. If you assume that you are what you want to be, your desire is fulfilled and, in fulfillment, all longing "to be" is neutralized. This, also, is an excellent check on yourself as to whether or not you have actually succeeded in changing self. You cannot continue desiring what has been realized. Rather, you are in a mood to give thanks for a gift received. Your desire is not something you labor to fulfill, it is recognizing something you already possess. It is assuming the feeling of being that which you desire to be.

Believing and being are one. The conceiver and his conception are one. Therefore, that which you conceive yourself to be can never be so far off as even to be near, for nearness implies separation. "If thou canst believe, all things are possible to him that believeth." Faith is the substance of things hoped for, the evidence of things not yet seen. If you assume that you are that finer, nobler one you wish to be, you will see others as they are related to your high assumption.

All enlightened men wish for the good of others. If it is the good of another you seek, you must use the same controlled contemplation. In meditation, you must represent the other to yourself as already being or having the greatness you desire for him. As for yourself, your desire for another must be an intense one. It is through desire that you rise above your present sphere and the road from longing to fulfillment is shortened as you experience in imagination all that you would experience in the flesh were you or your friend the embodiment of the desire you have for yourself or him. Experience has taught me that this is the perfect way to achieve my great goals for others as well as for myself. However, my own failures would convict me were I to imply that I have completely mastered the control of my attention. I can, however, with the ancient teacher say: "This one thing I do, forgetting those things which are behind, and reaching forth unto those things which are before – I press towards the mark for the prize."

Truth

I wish to ask each one of you listening to me today a question – a question which must be close to the hearts of us all concerning truth. If a man known to you as a murderer broke into your home and asked the whereabouts of your mother, would you tell him where she was? Would you tell him the truth? Would you? I venture not – I hope not. In the most mystical of the Gospels – in the Gospel of St. John we read, "Ye shall know the truth, and the truth shall make you free." Therein lies a challenge to us all, "The truth shall make you free." If you told the truth concerning your mother, would you set her free? Again, in John we read, "Sanctify them by the truth." If you gave your mother up to a murderer, would you "sanctify her?" What, then, is the truth of which the Bible so constantly speaks? The truth of the Bible is always coupled with love. The truth of the Bible is that spiritual realization of conscious life in God towards which the human soul evolves through all eternity.

Truth is an ever-increasing illumination. No one who seeks sincerely for truth need fear the outcome for every raising erstwhile truth brings into view some larger truth which it had hidden. The true seeker after truth is not a smug, critical, holier than thou person. Rather, the true seeker after truth knows the words of Zechariah to be true. "Speak ye every man the truth to his neighbor and let none of you imagine evil in your hearts against his neighbor." The seeker after truth does not judge from appearances – he sees the good, the truth in all he observes. He knows that a true judgment need not conform to the external reality to which it relates. Never are we so blind to the truth as when we see things as they seem to be. Only pictures that idealize really depict the truth. It is never superior insight but rather, purblindness that reads into the greatness of another some littleness with which it happens to be familiar.

We all know at least one petty gossip who not only imagines evil against his neighbor, but also insists upon spreading that evil far and wide. His cruel accusations are always accompanied by the statement, "It's a fact," or "I know it's the truth." How far from the truth he is. Even if it were the truth as he knows the truth, it is better not to voice it for "A truth told with bad intent beats all the lies you can invent." Such a man is not a seeker after the truth as revealed in the Bible. He seeks not truth so much as support for his own point of view. By his prejudices, he opens a door by which his enemies enter and make their own the secret places of his heart. Let us seek sincerely for the truth as Robert Browning expresses it:

"Truth is within ourselves; it take no rise

From outward things, whate'er you may believe.

There is an immortal center in us all

Where truth abides in fullness.

The truth that is within us is governed by imaginative love. Knowing this great truth, we can no longer imagine evil against any neighbor. We will imagine the best of our neighbor.

It is my belief that wherever man's attitude towards life is governed by imaginative love, there it is religious – there he worships – there he perceives the truth. I am going to speak on this subject next Sunday morning when my title will be, "Imaginative Love." At that time, I am to have the pleasure and the privilege of taking Dr. Frederick Bailes' service at the Fox Wilshire Theater on Wilshire Boulevard near La Cienega. The service will be held as Dr. Bailes always conducts it at 10:30 Sunday morning.

It is an intuitive desire of all mankind to be a finer, nobler being, to do the loving thing. But we can do the loving thing only when all we imagine is full of love for our neighbor. Then we know the truth, the truth that sets all mankind free. I believe this is a message that will aid us all in the art of living a better and finer life. Infinite love in unthinkable origin was called God, the Father. Infinite love in creative expression was called God, the Son. Infinite love in universal interpenetration, in Infinite Immanence, and in Eternal procession, was called God, the Holy Ghost. We must learn to know ourselves as Infinite Love, as good rather than evil. This is not something that we have to become; it is, rather, for us to recognize something that we are already.

The original birthplace of imagination is in love. Love is its lifeblood. Insofar as imagination retains its own life's blood, its visions are images of truth. Then it mirrors the living identity of the thing it beholds. But if imagination should deny the very power that has brought it to birth then the direst sort of horror will begin. Instead of rendering back living images of the truth, imagination will fly to love's opposite – fear and its visions will then be perverted and contorted reflections cast upon a screen of frightful fantasy. Instead of being the supremely creative power, it will become the active agent of destruction. Wherever man's attitude to life is truly imaginative, there man and God are merged in creative unity. Remember that Love is always creative, causative in every sphere from the highest to the very lowest. There never has existed thought, word or deed that was not caused by love, or by its opposite - fear of some kind, even if it were only a desire of a not very worthy aim. Love and fear are the mainspring of our mental machinery. Everything is a thought before it becomes a thing. I suggest the pursuit of a high ideal to make a fact of being become a fact of consciousness and to do this by training the imagination to realize that the only atmosphere in which we truly live and move and have our being is Infinite Love. God is Love. Love never faileth. Infinite Creative Spirit is Love. The urge that caused Infinite unconditioned consciousness to condition Itself into millions of sensitive forms is Love.

Love regarded as an abstraction - apart from an object - is unthinkable. Love is not love if there is no beloved. Love only becomes thinkable in relation, in process in act. Let us recognize with Blake that, "He who will not live by love must be subdued by fear," and set ourselves the highest of ideals to love and to live by. But our highest ideals do not bless unless they come down and take on flesh. We must make results and accomplishments the crucial test of our imagination and our love, for incarnation is the only true realization. Our faithfulness must be to the sum of all the truth we know and it must be absolute. Otherwise, that truth lacks a vehicle and cannot be incarnated in us.

Our concept of ourselves determines the scenery of our lives. We are ever our own jailers. The prison doors that we thought closed are truly ajar - waiting for us to see the truth. "Man ever surrounds himself with the true image of himself," said Emerson. "Every spirit builds itself a house and beyond its house, a world, and beyond its world, a heaven. Know then the world exists for you, for you the phenomenon is perfect. What we are that only can we see. All that Adam had, all the Caesar could, you have and can do."

Adam called his house heaven and earth. Caesar called his house, Rome. You perhaps call yours a cobbler's trade, or a hundred acres of land, or a scholar's garret. Yet line for line, and point for point, your dominion is as great as theirs, though without such fine names. Build, therefore, your own world and as fast as you conform your life to the pure idea in your mind, that will unfold its great proportions.

The truth is our secret inward reality, the cause, the meaning, the relation of our lives to all things. Let the truth carry us heavenwards, expanding our conceptions, increasing our understanding until we know the "Truth" and are made "Free."

At Your Command

Can man decree a thing and have it come to pass? Most decidedly he can! Man has always decreed that which has appeared in his world and is today decreeing that which is appearing in his world and shall continue to do so as long as man is conscious of being man. Not one thing has ever appeared in man's world but what man decreed that it should. This you may deny, but try as you will you cannot disprove it, for this decreeing is based upon a changeless principle. You do not command things to appear by your words or loud affirmations. Such vain repetition is more often than not confirmation of the opposite. Decreeing is ever done in consciousness. That is; every man is conscious of being that which he has decreed himself to be. The dumb man without using words is conscious of being dumb. Therefore he is decreeing himself to be dumb.

When the Bible is read in this light you will find it to be the greatest scientific book ever written. Instead of looking upon the Bible as the historical record of an ancient civilization or the biography of the unusual life of Jesus, see it as a great psychological drama taking place in the consciousness of man.

Claim it as your own and you will suddenly transform your world from the barren deserts of Egypt to the promised land of Canaan.

Every one will agree with the statement that all things were made by God, and without him there is nothing made that is made, but what man does not agree upon is the identity of God. All the churches and priesthoods of the world disagree as to the identity and true nature of God. The Bible proves beyond the shadow of a doubt that Moses and the prophets were in one hundred per cent accord as to the identity and nature of God. And Jesus' life and teachings are in agreement with the findings of the prophets of old. Moses discovered God to be man's awareness of being, when he declared these little understood words, "I AM hath sent me unto you." David sang in his psalms, "Be still and know that I AM God." Isaiah declared, "I AM the Lord and there is none else. There is no God beside me. I girded thee, though thou hast not known me. I form the light, and create darkness; I make peace, and create evil. I the Lord do all these things."

The awareness of being as God is stated hundreds of times in the New Testament. To name but a few: "I AM the shepherd, I AM the door; I AM the resurrection and the life; I AM the way; I AM the Alpha and Omega; I AM the beginning and the end"; and again, "Whom do you say that I AM?"

It is not stated, "I, Jesus, am the door. I, Jesus am the way," nor is it said, "Whom do you say that I, Jesus, am?" It is clearly stated, "I AM the way." The awareness of being is the door through which the manifestations of life pass into the world of form.

Consciousness is the resurrecting power – resurrecting that which man is conscious of being. Man is ever out-picturing that which he is conscious of being. This is the truth that makes man free, for man is always self-imprisoned or self-freed.

If you, the reader, will give up all of your former beliefs in a God apart from yourself, and claim God as your awareness of being – as Jesus and the prophets did – you will transform your world with the realization that, "I and my father are one." This statement, "I and my father are one, but my father is greater than I," seems very confusing – but if interpreted in the light of what we have just said concerning the identity of God, you will find it very revealing. Consciousness, being God, is as 'father.' The thing that you are conscious of being is the 'son' bearing witness of his 'father.' It is like the conceiver and its conceptions. The conceiver is ever greater than his conceptions yet ever remains one with his conception. For instance; before you are conscious of being man, you are first conscious of being. Then you become conscious of being man. Yet you remain as conceiver, greater than your conception – man.

Jesus discovered this glorious truth and declared himself to be one with God – not a God that man had fashioned. For he never recognized such a God. He said, "If any man should ever come, saying, 'Look here or look there,' believe them not, for the kingdom of God is within you." Heaven is within you. Therefore, when it is recorded that "He went unto his father," it is telling you that he rose in consciousness to the point where he was just conscious of being, thus transcending the limitations of his present conception of himself, called 'Jesus.'

In the awareness of being all things are possible, he said, "You shall decree a thing and it shall come to pass." This is his decreeing – rising in consciousness to the naturalness of being the thing desired. As he expressed it, "And I, if I be lifted up, I shall draw all men unto me." If I be lifted up in consciousness to the naturalness of the thing desired I will draw the manifestation of that desire unto me. For he states, "No man comes unto me save the father within me draws him, and I and my father are one." Therefore, consciousness is the father that is drawing the manifestations of life unto you.

You are, at this very moment, drawing into your world that which you are now conscious of being. Now you can see what is meant by, "You must be born again." If you are dissatisfied with your present expression in life the only way to change it, is to take your attention away form that which seems so real to you and rise in consciousness to that which you desire to be. You cannot serve two masters, therefore to take your attention from one state of consciousness and place it upon another is to die to one and live to the other.

The question, "Whom do you say that I AM?" is not addressed to a man called 'Peter' by one called 'Jesus.' This is the eternal question addressed to one's self by one's true being. In other words, "Whom do you say that you are?" For your conviction of yourself – your opinion of yourself will determine your expression in life. He states, "You believe in God – believe also in me." In other words, it is the me within you that is this God.

Praying then, is seen to be recognizing yourself to be that which you now desire, rather than its accepting form of petitioning a God that does not exist for that which you now desire.

So can't you see why the millions of prayers are unanswered? Men pray to a God that does not exist. For instance: To be conscious of being poor and to pray to a God for riches is to be rewarded with that which you are conscious of being – which is poverty. Prayers to be successful must be claiming rather than begging – so if you would pray for riches turn from your picture of poverty by denying the very evidence of your senses and assume the nature of being wealthy.

We are told, "When you pray go within in secret and shut the door. And that which your father sees in secret, with that will he reward you openly." We have identified the 'father' to be the awareness of being. We have also identified the 'door' to be the awareness of being. So 'shutting the door' is shutting out that which 'I' am now aware of being and claiming myself to be that which 'I' desire to be. The very moment my claim is established to the point of conviction, that moment I begin to draw unto myself the evidence of my claim.

Do not question the how of these things appearing, for no man knows that way. That is, no manifestation knows how the things desired will appear.

Consciousness is the way or door through which things appear. He said, "I AM the way" – not 'I,' John Smith, am the way, but "I AM," the awareness of being, is the way through which the thing shall come. The signs always follow. They never precede. Things have no reality other than in consciousness. Therefore, get the consciousness first and the thing is compelled to appear.

You are told, "Seek ye first the kingdom of Heaven and all things shall be added unto you." Get first the consciousness of the things that you are seeking and leave the things alone. This is what is meant by "Ye shall decree a thing and it shall come to pass."

Apply this principle and you will know what it is to 'prove me and see." The story of Mary is the story of every man. Mary was not a woman - giving birth in some miraculous way to one called 'Jesus.' Mary is the awareness of being that ever remains virgin, no matter how many desires it gives birth to. Right now look upon yourself as this virgin Mary - being impregnated by yourself through the medium of desire - becoming one with your desire to the point of embodying or giving birth to your desire.

For instance: It is said of Mary (whom you now know to be yourself) that she know not a man. Yet she conceived. That is, you, John Smith, have no reason to believe that that which you now desire is possible, but having discovered your awareness of being to be God, you make this awareness your husband and conceive a man child (manifestation) of the Lord, "For thy maker is thine husband; the Lord of hosts is his name; the Lord God of the whole earth shall he be called." Your ideal or ambition is this conception - the first command to her, which is now to yourself, is "Go, tell no man." That is, do not discuss your ambitions or desires with another for the other will only echo your present fears. Secrecy is the first law to be observed in realizing your desire.

The second, as we are told in the story of Mary, is to "Magnify the Lord." We have identified the Lord as your awareness of being. Therefore, to 'magnify the Lord' is to revalue or expand one's present conception of one's self to the point where this revaluation becomes natural. When this naturalness is attained you give birth by becoming that which you are one with in consciousness.

The story of creation is given us in digest form in the first chapter of John.

"In the beginning was the word." Now, this very second, is the 'beginning' spoken of. It is the beginning of an urge - a desire. 'The word' is the desire swimming around in your consciousness - seeking embodiment. The urge of itself has no reality, For, "I AM" or the awareness of being is the only reality. Things live only as long as I AM aware of being them; so to realize one's desire, the second line of this first verse of John must be applied. That is, "And the word was with God." The word, or desire, must be fixed or united with consciousness to give it reality. The awareness becomes aware of being the thing desired, thereby nailing itself upon the form or conception - and giving life unto its conception - or resurrecting that which was heretofore a dead or unfulfilled desire. "Two shall agree as touching anything and it shall be established on earth."

This agreement is never made between two persons. It is between the awareness and the thing desired. You are now conscious of being, so you are actually saying to yourself, without using words, "I AM." Now, if it is a state of health that you are desirous of attaining, before you have any evidence of health in your world, you begin to FEEL yourself to be healthy. And the very second the feeling "I AM healthy" is attained the two have agreed. That is, I AM and health have agreed to be one and this agreement ever results in the birth of a child which is the thing agreed upon – in this case, health. And because I made the agreement I express the thing agreed. So you can see why Moses stated, "I AM hath sent me." For what being, other than I AM could send you into expression? None – for "I AM the way – Beside me there is no other." If you take the wings of the morning and fly into the uttermost parts of the world or if you make your bed in Hell, you will still be aware of being. You are ever sent into expression by your awareness and your expression is ever that which you are aware of being.

Again, Moses stated, "I AM that I AM." Now here is something to always bear in mind. You cannot put new wine in old bottles or new patches upon old garments. That is; you cannot take with you into the new consciousness any part of the old man. All of your present beliefs, fears and limitations are weights that bind you to your present level of consciousness. If you would transcend this level you must leave behind all that is now your present self, or conception of yourself. To do this you take your attention away from all that is now your problem or limitation and dwell upon just being. That is; you say silently but feeling to yourself, "I AM. Do not condition this 'awareness' as yet. Just declare yourself to be, and continue to do so, until you are lost in the feeling of just being – faceless and formless. When this expansion of consciousness is attained, then, within this formless deep of yourself give form to the new conception by FEELING yourself to be THAT which you desire to be.

You will find within this deep of yourself all things to be divinely possible. Everything in the world which you can conceive of being, is to you, within this present formless awareness, a most natural attainment.

The invitation given us in the Scriptures is – "to be absent from the body and be present with the Lord." The 'body' being your former conception of yourself and 'the Lord' – your awareness of being. This is what is meant when Jesus said to Nicodemus, "Ye must be born again for except ye be born again ye cannot enter the kingdom of Heaven." That is; except you leave behind you your present conception of yourself and assume the nature of the new birth, you will continue to out-picture your present limitations.

The only way to change your expressions of life is to change your consciousness. For consciousness is the reality that eternally solidifies itself in the things round about you. Man's world in its every detail is his consciousness out-pictured. You can no more change your environment, or world, by destroying things than you can your reflection by destroying the mirror. Your environment, and all within it, reflects that which you are in consciousness. As long as you continue to be that in consciousness so long will you continue to out-picture it in your world.

Knowing this, begin to revalue yourself. Man has placed too little value upon himself. In the Book of Numbers you will read, "In that day there were giants in the land; and we were in our own sight as grasshoppers. And we were in their sight as grasshoppers." This does not mean a time in the dim past when man had the stature of giants. Today is the day, - the eternal now - when conditions round about you have attained the appearance of giants (such as unemployed, the armies of your enemy, your problems and all things that seem to threaten you) those are the giant that make you feel yourself to be a grasshopper. But, you are told, you were first, in your own sight a grasshopper and because of this you were to the giants – a grasshopper. In other words, you can only be to others what you are first to yourself. Therefore, to revalue yourself and begin to feel yourself to be the giant, a center of power, is to dwarf these former giants and make of them grasshoppers. "All the inhabitants of the earth are as nothing, and he doeth according to his will in the armies of Heaven and among all the inhabitants of the earth; and none can stay his hand, nor say unto him, "What doest thou'?" This being spoken of is not the orthodox God sitting in space but the one and only God – the everlasting father, your awareness of being. So awake to the power that you are, not as man, but as your true self, a faceless, formless awareness, and free yourself from your self imposed prison.

"I am the good shepherd and know my sheep and am known of mine. My sheep hear my voice and I know them and they will follow me." Awareness is the good shepherd. What I am aware of being, is the 'sheep' that follow me. So good a 'shepherd' is your awareness that it has never lost one of the 'sheep' that you are aware of being.

I am a voice calling in the wilderness of human confusion for such as I am aware of being, and never shall there come a time when that which I am convinced that I am shall fail to find me. "I AM" is an open door for all that I am to enter. Your awareness of being is lord and shepherd of your life. So, "The Lord is my shepherd; I shall not want" is seen in its true light now to be your consciousness. You could never be in want of proof or lack the evidence of that which you are aware of being.

This being true, why not become aware of being great; God-loving; wealthy; healthy; and all attributes that you admire?

It is just as easy to possess the consciousness of these qualities as it is to possess their opposites for you have not your present consciousness because of your world. On the contrary, your world is what it is because of your present consciousness. Simple, is it not? Too simple in fact for the wisdom of man that tries to complicate everything.

Paul said of this principle, "It is to the Greeks" (or wisdom of this world) "foolishness." "And to the Jews" (or those who look for signs) "a stumbling block"; with the result, that man continues to walk in darkness rather than awake to the being that he is. Man has so long worshipped the images of his own making that at first he finds this revelation blasphemous, since it spells death to all his previous beliefs in a God apart from himself. This revelation will bring the knowledge that "I and my father are one but my father is greater than I." You are one with your present conception of yourself. But you are greater than that which you are at present aware of being.

Before man can attempt to transform his world he must first lay the foundation - "I AM the Lord." That is, man's awareness, his consciousness of being is God. Until this is firmly established so that no suggestion or argument put forward by others can shake it, he will find himself returning to the slavery of his former beliefs. "If ye believe not that I AM he, ye shall die in your sins." That is, you shall continue to be confused and thwarted until you find the cause of your confusion. When you have lifted up the son of man then shall you know that I AM he, that is, that I, John Smith, do nothing of myself, but my father, or that state of consciousness which I am now one with does the works.

When this is realized every urge and desire that springs within you shall find expression in your world. "Behold I stand at the door and knock. If any man hear my voice and open the door I will come in to him and sup with him and he with me." The "I" knocking at the door is the urge.

The door is your consciousness. To open the door is to become one with that that which is knocking by FEELING oneself to be the thing desired. To feel one's desire as impossible is to shut the door or deny this urge expression. To rise in consciousness to the naturalness of the thing felt is to swing wide the door and invite this one into embodiment.

That is why it is constantly recorded that Jesus left the world of manifestation and ascended unto his father. Jesus, as you and I, found all things impossible to Jesus, as man. But having discovered his father to be the state of consciousness of the thing desired, he but left behind him the "Jesus consciousness" and rose in consciousness to that state desired and stood upon it until he became one with it. As he made himself one with that, he became that in expression.

This is Jesus simple message to man: Men are but garments that the impersonal being, I AM, - the presence that men call God - dwells in. Each garment has certain limitations. In order to transcend these limitations and give expression to that which, as man - John Smith - you find yourself incapable of doing, you take your attention away from your present limitations, or John Smith conception of yourself, and merge yourself in the feeling of being that which you desire. Just how this desire or newly attained consciousness will embody itself, no man knows. For I, or the newly attained consciousness, has ways that ye know not of; its ways are past finding out. Do not speculate as to the HOW of this consciousness embodying itself, for no man is wise enough to know the how. Speculation is proof that you have not attained to the naturalness of being the thing desired and so are filled with doubts.

You are told, "He who lacks wisdom let him ask of God, that gives to all liberally, and upbraideth not; and it shall be given unto him. But let him ask not doubting for he who doubts is as a wave of the sea that is tossed and battered by the winds. And let not such a one think that he shall receive anything from the Lord." You can see why this statement is made, for only upon the rock of faith can anything be established. If you have not the consciousness of the thing you have not the cause or foundation upon which thing is erected.

A proof of this established consciousness is given you in the words, "Thank you, father." When you come into the joy of thanksgiving so that you actually feel grateful for having received that which is not yet apparent to the senses, you have definitely become one in consciousness with the thing for which you gave thanks. God (your awareness) is not mocked. You are ever receiving that which you are aware of being and no man gives thanks for something which he has not received. "Thank you father" is not, as it is used by many today a sort of magical formula. You need never utter aloud the words, "Thank you, father." In applying this principle as you rise in consciousness to the point where you are really grateful and happy for having received the thing desired, you automatically rejoice and give thanks inwardly. You have already accepted the gift which was but a desire before you rose in consciousness, and your faith is now the substance that shall clothe your desire.

This rising in consciousness is the spiritual marriage where two shall agree upon being one and their likeness or image is established on earth.

"For whatsoever ye ask in my name the same give I unto you." 'Whatsoever' is quite a large measure. It is the unconditional. It does not state if society deems it right or wrong that you should ask it, it rests with you. Do you really want it? Do you desire it? That is all that is necessary. Life will give it to you if you ask 'in his name.'

His name is not a name that you pronounce with the lips. You can ask forever in the name of God or Jehovah or Christ Jesus and you will ask in vain. 'Name' means nature; so, when you ask in the nature of a thing, results ever follow. To ask in the name is to rise in consciousness and become one in nature with the thing desired, rise in consciousness to the nature of the thing, and you will become that thing in expression. Therefore, "what things soever ye desire, when ye pray, believe that ye receive them and ye shall receive them."

Praying, as we have shown you before, is recognition – the injunction to believe that ye receive is first person, present tense. This means that you must be in the nature of the things asked for before you can receive them.

To get into the nature easily, general amnesty is necessary. We are told, "Forgive if ye have aught against any, that your father also, which is in Heaven, may forgive you. But if ye forgive not, neither will your father forgive you." This may seem to be some personal God who is pleased or displeased with your actions but this is not the case.

Consciousness, being God, if you hold in consciousness anything against man, you are binding that condition in your world. But to release man from all condemnation is to free yourself so that you may rise to any level necessary; there is therefore, no condemnation to those in Christ Jesus.

Therefore, a very good practice before you enter into your meditation is first to free every man in the world from blame. For LAW is never violated and you can rest confidently in the knowledge that every man's conception of himself is going to be his reward. So you do not have to bother yourself about seeing whether or not man gets what you consider he should get. For life makes no mistakes and always gives man that which man first gives himself.

This brings us to that much abused statement of the Bible on tithing. Teachers of all kinds have enslaved man with this affair of tithing, for not themselves understanding the nature of tithing and being themselves fearful of lack, they have led their followers to believe that a tenth part of their income should be given to the Lord. Meaning, as they make very clear, that, when one gives a tenth part of his income to their particular organization he is giving his "tenth part" to the Lord - (or is tithing). But remember, "I AM" the Lord." Your awareness of being is the God that you give to and you ever give in this manner.

Therefore when you claim yourself to be anything, you have given that claim or quality to God. And your awareness of being, which is no respecter of persons, will return to you pressed down, shaken together, and running over with that quality or attribute which you claim for yourself.

Awareness of being is nothing that you could ever name. To claim God to be rich; to be great; to be love; to be all wise; is to define that which cannot be defined. For God is nothing that could ever be named.

Tithing is necessary and you do tithe with God. But from now on give to the only God and see to it that you give him the quality that you desire as man to express by claiming yourself to be the great, the wealthy, the loving, the all wise.

Do not speculate as to how you shall express these qualities or claims, for life has a way that you, as man, know not of. Its ways are past finding out. But, I assure you, the day you claim these qualities to the point of conviction, your claims will be honored. There is nothing covered that shall not be uncovered. That which is spoken in secret shall be proclaimed from the housetops. That is, your secret convictions of yourself - these secret claims that no man knows of, when really believed, will be shouted from the housetops in your world. For your convictions of yourself are the words of the God within you, which words are spirit and cannot return unto you void but must accomplish whereunto they are sent.

You are at this moment calling out of the infinite that which you are now conscious of being. And not one word or conviction will fail to find you.

"I AM" the vine and ye are the branches." Consciousness is the 'vine,' and those qualities which you are now conscious of being are as 'branches' that you feed and keep alive. Just as a branch has no life except it be rooted in the vine, so likewise things have no life except you be conscious of them. Just as a branch withers and dies if the sap of the vine ceases to flow towards it, so do things in your world pass away if you take your attention from them, because your attention is as the sap of life that keeps alive and sustains the things of your world.

To dissolve a problem that now seems so real to you all that you do is remove your attention from it. In spite of its seeming reality, turn from it in consciousness. Become indifferent and begin to feel yourself to be that which would be the solution of the problem.

For instance; if you were imprisoned no man would have to tell you that you should desire freedom. Freedom, or rather the desire of freedom would be automatic. So why look behind the four walls of your prison bars? Take your attention from being imprisoned and begin to feel yourself to be free. FEEL it to the point where it is natural – the very second you do so, those prison bars will dissolve. Apply this same principle to any problem.

I have seen people who were in debt up to their ears apply this principle and in the twinkling of an eye debts that were mountainous were removed. I have seen those whom doctors had given up as incurable take their attention away from their problem of disease and begin to feel themselves to be well in spite of the evidence of their sense to the contrary. In no time at all this so called "incurable disease" vanished and left no scar.

Your answer to, "Whom do you say that I AM"? [sic] ever determines your expression. As long as you are conscious of being imprisoned or diseased, or poor, so long will you continue to out-picture or express these conditions.

When man realized that he is now that which he is seeking and begins to claim that he is, he will have the proof of his claim. This cue is given you in words, "Whom seek ye?" And they answered, "Jesus." And the voice said, "I am he." 'Jesus' here means salvation or savior. You are seeking to be salvaged from that which is not your problem.

"I am" is he that will save you. If you are hungry, your savior is food. If you are poor, your savior is riches. If you are imprisoned, your savior is freedom. If you are diseased, it will not be a man called Jesus who will save you, but health will become your savior. Therefore, claim "I am he," in other words, claim yourself to be the thing desired. Claim it in consciousness – not in words – and consciousness will reward you with your claim. You are told, "You shall find me when you FEEL after me." Well, FEEL after that quality in consciousness until you FEEL yourself to be it. When you lose yourself in the feeling of being it, the quality will embody itself in your world.

You are healed from your problem when you touch the solution of it. "Who has touched me? For I perceive virtue is gone out of me." Yes, the day you touch this being within you – FEELING yourself to be cured or healed, virtues will come out of your very self and solidify themselves in your world as healings.

It is said, 'You believe in God. Believe also in me for I am he." Have the faith of God. "He made himself one with God and found it not robbery to do the works of God." Go you and do likewise. Yes, begin to believe your awareness, your consciousness of being to be God. Claim for yourself all the attributes that you have heretofore given an external God and you will begin to express these claims.

"For I am not a God afar off. I am nearer than your hands and feet – nearer than your very breathing." I am your awareness of being. I am that in which all that I shall ever be aware of being shall begin and end. "For before the world was I AM; and when the world shall cease to be, I AM; before Abraham was, I AM." This I AM is your awareness.

"Except the Lord build the house they labor in vain that build it." 'The Lord,' being your consciousness, except that which you seek is first established in your consciousness, you will labor in vain to find it. All things must begin and end in consciousness.

So, blessed indeed is the man that trusteth in himself – for man's faith in God will ever be measured by his confidence in himself. You believe in a God, believe also in ME.

Put not your trust in men for men but reflect the being that you are, and can only bring to you or do unto you that which you have first done unto yourself.

"No man taketh away my life, I lay it down myself." I have the power to lay it down and the power to take it up again.

No matter what happens to man in this world it is never an accident. It occurs under the guidance of an exact and changeless Law.

"No man" (manifestation) "comes unto me except the father within me draw him," and "I and my father are one." Believe this truth and you will be free. Man has always blamed others for that which he is and will continue to do so until he find himself as cause of all. "I AM" comes not to destroy but to fulfill. "I AM," the awareness within you, destroys nothing but ever fill full the molds or conception one has of one's self.

It is impossible for the poor man to find wealth in this world no matter how he is surrounded with it until he first claims himself to be wealthy. For signs follow, they do not precede. To constantly kick and complain against the limitations of poverty while remaining poor in consciousness is to play the fool's game. Changes cannot take place from that level of consciousness for life in constantly out-picturing all levels.

Follow the example of the prodigal son. Realize that you, yourself brought about this condition of waste and lack and make the decision within yourself to rise to a higher level where the fatted calf, the ring, and the robe await your claim.

There was no condemnation of the prodigal when he had the courage to claim this inheritance as his own. Others will condemn us only as long as we continue in that for which we condemn ourselves. So: "Happy is the man that condemneth himself not in that which he alloweth." For to life nothing is condemned. All is expressed.

Life does not care whether you call yourself rich or poor; strong or weak. It will eternally reward you with that which you claim as true of yourself.

The measurements of right and wrong belong to man alone. To life there is nothing right or wrong. As Paul stated in his letters to the Romans: "I know and am persuaded by the Lord Jesus that there is nothing unclean of itself, but to him that esteemeth anything to be unclean, to him it is unclean." Stop asking yourself whether you are worthy or unworthy to receive that which you desire. You, as man, did not create the desire. Your desires are ever fashioned within you because of what you now claim yourself to be.

When a man is hungry, (without thinking) he automatically desires food. When imprisoned, he automatically desires freedom and so forth. Your desires contain within themselves the plan of self-expression.

So leave all judgments out of the picture and rise in consciousness to the level of your desire and make yourself one with it by claiming it to be so now. For: "My grace is sufficient for thee. My strength is made perfect in weakness."

Have faith in this unseen claim until the conviction is born within you that it is so. Your confidence in this claim will pay great rewards. Just a little while and he, the thing desired, will come. But without faith it is impossible to realize anything. Through faith the worlds were framed because "faith is the substance of the thing hoped for – the evidence of the thing not yet seen."

Don't be anxious or concerned as to results. They will follow just as surely as day follows night.

Look upon your desires – all of them – as the spoken words of God, and every word or desire a promise. The reason most of us fail to realize our desires is because we are constantly conditioning them. Do not condition your desire. Just accept it as it comes to you. Give thanks for it to the point that you are grateful for having already received it – then go about your way in peace.

Such acceptance of your desire is like dropping seed – fertile seed – into prepared soil. For when you can drop the thing desired in consciousness, confident that it shall appear, you have done all that is expected to you. But, to be worried or concerned about the HOW of your desire maturing is to hold these fertile seeds in a mental grasp, and, therefore, never to have dropped them in the soil of confidence.

The reason men condition their desires is because they constantly judge after the appearance of being and see the things as real – forgetting that the only reality is the consciousness back of them.

To see things as real is to deny that all things are possible to God. The man who is imprisoned and sees his four walls as real is automatically denying the urge or promise of God within him of freedom.

A question often asked when this statement is made is; If one's desire is a gift of God how can you say that if one desires to kill a man that such a desire is good and therefore God sent? In answer to this let me say that no man desires to kill another. What he does desire is to be freed from such a one. But because he does not believe that the desire to be free from such a one contains within itself the powers of freedom, he conditions that desire and sees the only way to express such freedom is to destroy the man – forgetting that the life wrapped within the desire has ways that he, as man, knows not of. Its ways are past finding out. Thus man distorts the gifts of God through his lack of faith.

Problems are the mountains spoken of that can be removed if one has but the faith of a grain of a mustard seed. Men approach their problem as did the old lady who, on attending service and hearing the priest say, "If you had but the faith of a grain of a mustard seed you would say unto yonder mountain 'be thou removed' and it shall be removed and nothing is impossible to you."

That night as she said her prayers, she quoted this part of the scriptures and retired to bed in what she thought was faith. On arising in the morning she rushed to the window and exclaimed: "I knew that old mountain would still be there."

For this is how man approaches his problem. He knows that they are still going to confront him. And because life is no respecter of persons and destroys nothing, it continues to keep alive that which he is conscious of being.

Things will disappear only as man changes in consciousness. Deny it if you will, it still remains a fact that consciousness is the only reality and things but mirror that which you are in consciousness. So the heavenly state you are seeking will be found only in consciousness, for the kingdom of heaven is within you. As the will of heaven is ever done on earth you are today living in the heaven that you have established within you. For here on this very earth your heaven reveals itself. The kingdom of heaven really is at hand. NOW is the accepted time. So create a new heaven, enter into a new state of consciousness and a new earth will appear.

"The former things shall pass away. They shall not be remembered not come into mind any more. For behold, I," (your consciousness) "come quickly and my reward is with me."

I am nameless but will take upon myself every name (nature) that you call me. Remember it is you, yourself, that I speak of as 'me.' So every conception that you have of yourself – that is every deep conviction – you have of yourself is that which you shall appear as being – for I AM not fooled; God is not mocked.

Now let me instruct you in the art of fishing. It is recorded that the disciples fished all night and caught nothing. Then Jesus came upon the scene and told them to cast their nets in once more, into the same waters that only a moment before were barren – and this time their nets were bursting with the catch.

This story is taking place in the world today right within you, the reader. For you have within you all the elements necessary to go fishing. But until you find that Jesus Christ, (your awareness) is Lord, you will fish, as did these disciples, in the night of human darkness. That is, you will fish for THINGS thinking things to be real and will fish with the human bait – which is a struggle and an effort – trying to make contact with this one and that one: trying to coerce this being or the other being; and all such effort will be in vain. But when you discover your awareness of being to be Christ Jesus you will let him direct your fishing. And you will fish in consciousness for the things that you desire. For your desire – will be the fish that you will catch, because your consciousness is the only living reality you will fish in the deep waters of consciousness.

If you would catch that which is beyond your present capacity you must launch out into deeper waters, for, within your present consciousness such fish or desires cannot swim. To launch out into deeper waters, you leave behind you all that is now your present problem, or limitation, by taking your ATTENTION AWAY from it. Turn your back completely upon every problem and limitation that you now possess.

Dwell upon just being by saying, "I AM," "I AM," "I AM," to yourself. Continue to declare to yourself that you just are. Do not condition this declaration, just continue to FEEL yourself to be and without warning you will find yourself slipping the anchor that tied you to the shallow of your problems and moving out into the deep.

This is usually accompanied with the feeling of expansion. You will FEEL yourself expand as though you were actually growing. Don't be afraid, for courage is necessary. You are not going to die to anything by your former limitations, but they are going to die as you move away from them, for they live only in your consciousness. In this deep or expanded consciousness you will find yourself to be a power that you had never dreamt of before.

The things desired before you shoved off from the shores of limitation are the fish you are going to catch in this deep. Because you have lost all consciousness of your problems and barriers, it is now the easiest thing in the world to FEEL yourself to be one with the things desired.

Because I AM (your consciousness) is the resurrection and the life, you must attach this resurrecting power that you are to the thing desired if you would make it appear and live in your world. Now you begin to assume the nature of the thing desired by feeling, "I AM wealthy"; "I AM free"; "I AM strong." When these 'FEELS' are fixed within yourself, your formless being will take upon itself the forms of the things felt. You become 'crucified' upon the feelings of wealth, freedom, and strength. - Remain buried in the stillness of these convictions. Then, as a thief in the night and when you least expect it, theses qualities will be resurrected in your world as living realities.

The world shall touch you and see that you are flesh and blood for you shall begin to bear fruit of the nature of these qualities newly appropriated. This is the art of successful fishing for the manifestations of life.

Successful realization of the thing desired is also told us in the story of Daniel in the lion's den. Here, it is recorded that Daniel, while in the lion's den, turned his back upon the lions and looked towards the light coming from above; that the lions remained powerless and Daniel's faith in his God saved him.

This also is your story and you too must do as Daniel did. If you found yourself in a lion's den you would have no other concern but lions. You would not be thinking of one thing in the world but your problem - which problem would be lions.

Yet, you are told that Daniel turned his back upon them and looked towards the light that was his God. If we would follow the example of Daniel we would, while imprisoned within the den of poverty of sickness, take our attention away from our problems of debts or sickness and dwell upon the thing we seek.

If we do not look back in consciousness to our problems but continue in faith – believing ourselves to be that which we seek, we too will find our prison walls open and the thing sought – yes, "whatsoever things" – realized.

Another story is told us; of the widow and the three drops of oil. The prophet asked the widow, "What have ye in your house?" And she replied, "Three drops of oil." He then said to her, "Go borrow vessels. Close the door after ye have returned into your house and begin to pour." And she poured from three drops of oil into all the borrowed vessels, filling them to capacity with oil remaining.

You, the reader, are this widow. You have not a husband to impregnate you or make you fruitful, for a 'widow' is a barren state. Your awareness is now the Lord – or the prophet that has become your husband.

Follow the example of the widow, who instead of recognizing an emptiness or nothingness, recognized the something – three drops of oil.

Then the command to her, "Go within and close the door," that is, shut the door of the senses that tell you of the empty measures, the debts, the problems.

When you have taken your attention away completely by shutting out the evidence of the senses, begin to FEEL the joy, - (symbolized by oil) - of having received the things desired. When the agreement is established within you so that all doubts and fears have passed away, then, you too will fill all the empty measures of your life and ill have an abundance running over.

Recognition is the power that conjures in the world. Every state that you have ever recognized, you have embodied. That which you are recognizing as true of yourself today is that which you are experiencing. So be as the widow and recognize joy, no matter how little the beginnings of recognition, and you will be generously rewarded – for the world is a magnified mirror, magnifying everything that you are conscious of being.

"I AM the Lord the God, which has brought thee out of the land of Egypt, out of the house of bondage; thou shalt have no other gods before me." What a glorious revelation, your awareness now revealed as the Lord thy God! Come, awake from your dream of being imprisoned. Realize that the earth is yours, "and the fullness thereof; the world, and all that dwells therein."

You have become so enmeshed in the belief that you are man that you have forgotten the glorious being that you are. Now with your memory restored DECREE the unseen to appear and it SHALL appear, for all things are compelled to respond to the Voice of God, Your awareness of being – the world is AT YOUR COMMAND!

CPSIA information can be obtained at www.ICGtesting.com
Printed in the USA
BVOW02s1427111213

338814BV00003B/648/P